I Never Wanted to be a Poet

David DeWitte

BookLeaf Publishing

India | USA | UK

Presentation by *BookLeaf Publishing*

Web: www.bookleafpub.com

E-mail: info@bookleafpub.com

ISBN: 9789363314191

First edition 2024

I dedicate this to my Daughter, the only thing of worth I have ever created.

ACKNOWLEDGEMENT

I would like to thank my Muse for creative inspiration, the spark that takes over and writes what the heart feels, and the brain refuses to think.

I would like to thank my family for supporting me through the good, the bad, and everything in between. Thank you for always seeing the good in me and encouraging me to grow and follow my dreams. Thank you for always loving me.

Four Letter Word

Love is such a simple four-letter word. Any two-year-old can say it; some may even be able to construct it, given they are provided the proper magnetic letters. Plastic toys that stick to the refrigerator.

Essentially teaching a child to view the world. Learning to think verbally so that they can describe objectively and ask questions that will solidify their individuality. Easy to understand at such a young age.

Funny how life complicates things. Each layer slowly buries the last until the weight is so heavy that you feel as if your heart may collapse.

This may actually be possible. People die all the time. Heart problems. Physical failure from emotional distress.

As a child, we are pure. We know and feel with absolute honesty. We dream and imagine and somehow stay grounded in both the physical and spiritual.

Our divinity isn't destroyed until we have lived long enough to pollute it with education and technological advances that distract and indoctrinate. We learn through memory rather than being taught to think.

Love requires no thought. No decision. No memory. It just is or it isn't. Time no longer exists. The continuum dwells somewhere in the ether. Exists outside of reality yet lives in the hearts and souls of the lovers and loved.

I am grown, a man in full, yet a child at heart. In my mind's eye, my heart, and soul, I know what love is. I have felt the effects both awesome and terrible.

My heart has been filled with an abundance of joy. So full that little bits and pieces would burst from every pore. I've literally sprinkled and showered the world with the love I've felt from others.

My heart has been shattered. Completely obliterated to nothing but dust. Perhaps even broken to the point that all that remained were atoms and subatomic particles.

Each time I knew that reconstructing would be impossible. I've never been much of a handyman. The art of kintsugi, while beautiful, the craft is beyond my aptitude.

If I had been born in Japan, perhaps beauty and simplicity would have taught me much. Rituals create stability and perfection.

Instead, I just fumble through the mundane. Eventually, the universe puts things in perspective. The heart mends itself.

Love. I know its definition. Truly and intimately. Know that it is the act of servitude. To put another's needs above one's own. It can exist in many different forms. Each the same, but somehow unique.

In essence, love is plural, polyamorous. Always. It's not a choice. It just is. You get to love more than once, never confined to singular. You can love both mother and father equally and in different ways. Offspring will have different and challenging traits. They will make poor decisions and even hate you at times. Still, love abounds. Once loved, always loved. Time and situations change nothing.

If you live long enough, you will love multiple partners. Perhaps at different times. Maybe even at once. Their mind may tell them it's impossible. For them, love is something else. An idea that was taught. Modern pollution of simplicity.

Love is simple. Love is hard. Love can be felt and expressed. Can feel like being dipped in the essence of God and the fires of hell. You serve; you get to be served. The good, the bad, and the terrible.

To live without love is to never live at all. To die with love is to live eternal. You will forever live in the hearts and memories of the ones left behind. Your passage to the unknown will be lit with their tears and the radiance you fill them with.

Simplified Complexity

I remember when life was simple, a small hand
wrapped in one
much larger. Impossible to see all the dangers,
the world large,
eyes small. Adults responsible for protection and
safekeeping
while young eyes absorb the world as a whole.

As children, we see through a different lens.
Plants, animals, dirt, creation,
people—all unique. Painted in different shades
and colors. Humans are
either adults or children. The color of our skin
doesn't faze the judgment
of a 6-year-old.

At that age, no concept of Nintendo or Xbox.
That idea hasn't even formed as
a concept, far from reality.
Kids walked home from school, pretended they
didn't have any homework,
that is, if they had parental guidance at that hour.
Mostly, parents worked, child
care an imagined luxury. One day… maybe.

Afternoons meant freedom, riding bikes, hiding
and seeking, playing some sort
of game with good guys and bad guys. Cops and
robbers, cowboys and Indians.
Sticks transform into swords, guns, bows, and
arrows. Imagination—it's all in the
eye of the stick-holder.

In a town of a million people, most sane citizens
avoided our neighborhood at
night. When the sun lit the sky, car doors
remained locked, as if thieves break into cars
traveling at 45 miles per hour.
Ethnicity was a hodgepodge of 50 shades of tan
with a sprinkle of melanin
deficient. At that level of poverty, we were all
equals. Surviving on instinct and pipe dreams.

Gangs protected neighborhoods and the people
that lived there regardless of
pigment. In a city this large, no one knows
everyone. Not even in their own
neighborhood. In fact, people mostly minded
their business. Anything less would be a sign of
disrespect. An outsider was obvious. Postures
and comfort, always noticeably different.

Gunshots, helicopters, spotlights, arguments in
the street—as common as roaches. 2 Live Crew

in a boombox, bounced down the street.
Bandanas and 40s dancing around a Weber grill.
A crazy redhead, firecracker with pale skin—
mother. She let them have it. Obscene music,
inappropriate for her babies. They apologized.
Yes, ma'am and all.
We hid, embarrassed.

Wasn't until later, time does these things. Money
changes things, perspectives, common sense.
Not that we had any, definitely not enough.
Money, not sense; there is nothing common
about sense. Poverty comes in layers.
Still poor, just not in the dirt.

I knew all the colors of the rainbow at 3 years
old. Crayons in a box, easier to recognize than
black and white. At some point, a line is drawn,
not hate, just no longer the same. I didn't
understand at 11 years of age,
perhaps I still don't.

I just know deep in my heart that hate is wrong.
Society is failing itself. Equality is a right. The
gold makes the rules; the other 99 percent scrape
and slave away. We fight over skin color,
identities, the adjectives, descriptions of how we
love or view ourselves on the inside. Peasants
judging peasants and condemning love. The

puppet masters pulling strings, counting coins,
manipulating sheep.

How I wish the world could see through those
eyes. So small. So true. Why do we allow our
differences to feed a fire we didn't start? Guard
your tongue. Cultivate what you project to your
children. We are born to love. Taught to hate.
Encouraged to squabble, all part of the plan. We
will forever be sheep as long as we eat from the
trough, allowing ourselves to be guided by a
corporate shepherd.

I remember when life was simple. My small
hand wrapped in one much larger, protection
from dangers I didn't believe in.
I remember when people were just people.
A time when you could ride your bike until the
streetlights came on.
Society was binary—adults and children.

Alone in the Dark

Some people are afraid of the dark.
Perhaps it makes them feel too much.
The night has a sound of its own.
That is, if you know what to listen for.
Tiny vibrations, the quiet.
That's when the muse speaks.
Tugs the tiny heartstring.
Guides the soul through the journey.
Everything always comes to life.
Stars dance in the sky.
Trees wiggle and wobble.
Shadows becoming tangible.
I've been that soul, am that soul.
Never lost, not quite wandering.
Some people just exist as creatures.
Survive while accepting what is expected.
Willing to march off to public education.
Work and eat and reproduce.
Spend a few hours watching TV.
Shows that we refer to as programs.
So obvious that it hides in plain sight.
Fingers searching for clickbait.
Smartphones for the masses.
Free with food stamps.
Depressed, anxious, addicted.

Safe in the light.
Groundhog Day every day.
Nothing more than a caged animal.
A dog that knows a few tricks.
So, I search—not searched, but search.
That is my purpose.
Life is neutral; existence has no meaning.
One must assign such on their own.
I looked for God in man's written pages.
In man's religious organizations.
Believed he existed as a child.
Knew he was real.
The creator of the universe wouldn't
hide in anything pedestrian and
archaic, nothing man-made.
Learned that belief means nothing.
People believe both fact and fiction.
Fiction is called make-believe for a reason.
Reality is tangible, empirical.
Facts don't care what you believe.
I became empty.
I obsessed over science.
Searched for answers.
Funny when you think about it.
People don't even remember their birth.
How can we discover the beginning of
something much, much older, something
from before recorded history?
I realized science isn't history.

Time, matter, space all began at once.
There was no before.
Something outside of this continuum influenced
this.
Cause and effect still existed on another plane.
This wasn't an accident.
Everything was created.
There is a creator.
People always knew this and practiced in
different ways.
It's always been obvious.
I think it was easier to see when we slept under
the stars,
when we had to hunt and gather.
The complexity surrounding us used to be
natural, not man-made.
Perhaps we have convinced ourselves of our
greatness.
As if people actually create from nothing.
All of man's creations are built from matter.
Even our thoughts are elemental.
Realization suddenly self-evident.
I became a blank canvas.
I became the painter.
The creator and the creation.
My brush and pen were provided.
I searched inward.
Found peace in the night.
Wrapped myself in the dark.

Found comfort in solitude.
Learned to know myself.
I've looked in the mirror.
Walked through the looking glass.
Eaten of the fruit and was unashamed.
It matters, not what others think.
To ponder such is a waste.
Life is so fragile, so precious.
Happiness is not a static state.
Some object that can be attained.
Few would even recognize it.
Society has traded joy for pleasure.
Sex, drugs, shopping, likes on social media.
Little spikes of dopamine.
Pleasure is not happiness.
Joy is not temporary.
Life is simple.
The answers are all around you.
All you have to do is sit alone in the dark.
Become friends with the person inside.
Know yourself, and the path will be obvious.
Follow your heart, your muse.
Never waste a breath.
The next could be your last.

Searching for a Showdown

Searching for a showdown, some sign
that I'm here, now, present.
Not just some illusion, ones and zeros
programmed into the matrix, a
hologram.

Stardust lights the field as I march off
into the abyss, chasing a shadow that's
cloaked by the moonless night.

Great men stand above, granting permission
to dance, the tune predetermined.
Freewill as illusionary as my reflection in a
pond.
Choices always limited and manufactured.
Decisions based on the only information known.

As a child, one resents many things.
Time felt infinite.
Parental responsibility felt unfulfilled.
Questions answered nothing.
Time spent guided by strangers, much longer
than family.
Craving the old game of catch.
Father always working in some distant place.

Home on the weekends.
Sometimes.

Latchkey kids, we'd walk home.
Three brothers.
The oldest, too young to take care of himself.
That child grew up to be me, whoever that is.

Sometimes I climbed a ladder, my stairway to
heaven.
An old, rusty fire escape, bolted to brick and
mortar.
Tall, but not high enough.
The clouds looked down, laughing at my
ignorance,
a cigarette burned between my fingers.

I'd sit and think, take a puff, but like Clinton, I
didn't inhale.
Not by choice but ignorance. I'd ponder the
wrongs.
Dream of futures never to come.
The itch in my soul, nagging like poison ivy.
I'll be a good dad, white picket and all.
Saddle soap to soften gloves.
I'll remember my lessons.
How and what to do with children.
My offspring. My family.

Never understanding the struggle.
Working long hours for peasant's wages.
Responsible for food and shelter.
Trading time for dollars.
Family never neglected but slaved to protect.
I know now, sad and shamed.
I'll never be that good.
Couldn't fill the boots left before me.

So, I search myself, the stars,
beg the earth mother for guidance.
The past written in stone.
The future promises nothing.
If by chance, however minute,
I can grow, bust out of this cocoon.
I'll do better.
I know now what life is.
The struggle.
I may not fill the old boots.
Know that I can't.
Our paths are different.
The world has evolved.
If I'm really here, I'll march on.
I may falter, fall, make mistakes more often than
not.
My prayer is not to remove failure but to be
judged on intent.

I will find balance, walk the tightrope, and reflect love.

Bedridden

I sit in the dark. Listening to the quiet.
The tick-tick-ticking of
time slipping away.
Sober in solitude.
Bedridden in a prison constructed of
perverse thoughts and
distorted memories.
Craving chemical enhancements to
reality.

Buddha is a god.
Not because of some magical powers,
but because of his ability to look inward and find
peace while experiencing the endless suffering
of the
world.

I am no god.
No Buddha.
Just a man.
Weak-minded yet strong in my ability to believe
in anything,
be it physical or dreamscape.

What is reality, really?

A thought, a feeling, something accessible by
our senses?
I see it, I hear it, I think it, I believe it.
The paradigm ensues.

For me, at this moment, it's this bed,
as I sift through these thoughts.
It's been three years since I quit.
Three years of purification, sobriety.
I did it; I'm the 1 per cent.
The best of the best.
Or am I?

What is success?
How can I quantify it?
There must be more to it than blending in.
Marching off to work.
Living in homes and driving cars I can't afford.

At least I look good on paper.
The other sheep can sleep easy, knowing
I'm reformed and in this bed.

The only real change that I've noticed,
in me anyway, is I can finally feel.
Truly feel again.
I hate it.

How can anyone choose this when they know.

One drop is all that's needed.
Better living through chemistry, or so they said.
But better how?
Better for society or better for a mind that can't
cope?

The weight of the world, oppressive.
One push of the plunger would put to sleep this
sick orchestra playing in my head.
Memories and futures instantly lulled into
comatose.
Limbs and breath as heavy as the weight once
was.

And should I slip into the great unknown.
Well, just know, whatever's next,
I come in peace.
Food for thought in a starving mind.
But rest assured, this too shall pass.

Tiny footprints can lead nowhere or march on.
These feet will eventually climb out of this bed.
The party of pity will end.
All things must run their course.
I will write, I will feel, and I will endure all
things.
The struggle builds character.
A mind stubborn enough to choose life, choose
pain,

just might be crazy enough to create other
realities.
Other feelings.

I am in the present.
I am free.
I will make it happen on my terms.
I am not Buddha.
I am no god.
I will not be chained and bedridden.
I will conduct my own orchestra.
I will be remembered when they sift through the
ashes.
I will leave all my obstacles burning in my
wake.

Perfectly Broken

She was, and then she wasn't.
A ghost in the rearview.
I can still feel her.
The glass slipping from my fingers.
Shattered to pieces.
Eyes seeing, always remembered.

At night I dream, little drops of sunshine.
A candlelit depression.
Aimless adventures.
Walking down no-name roads in paper towns.
A parallel existence.

I sleep when not needed.
Craving the dreamscape.
Pills in a rainbow of colors.
Pharmaceutical clouds to float down rivers.
A fantasy timeshare to infinity.

Waking hours wading through reservations.
Deprived of everything except sleep.
A zombie walking.
Waiting for the last bell.
Father Time must be lonely.

The hours always tick-tocking away.
Fingers grasping.
Always coming up empty.
Hand in the cookie jar.
Closed mouth dying to be fed.
Searching for anything.

Pain, just another feeling.
Pleasure, a welcome distraction.
Selling my body for emotional currency.
Paid for with shame and stained sheets.

There was a moment.
The stars aligned and the
disgusting act of free use became beauty.
Time stopped for a breath.
Nothing mattered.
Milk spilled with no tears.

In the aftermath, shower hot, not enough soap.
Filthy little thing.
Lost in the moment, working on disinfection.
Success in the forgotten glass.
Perfectly broken

The Cost of Love

My heart hurts. Each beat feels like it could be
my last.
Ripping through my soul.
Skin on fire, each pore electric.
I sit in this fire, torn and broken
Unable to swallow a morsel of substance
My pride humbled, crushed, and bruised
I hate it but endure out of necessity.
I know that to no longer hurt is to let go of the
love.
So, I wear this pain as a trophy.
My badge of honor.
To love harder, endure more, and never forget.
Hope lives in this pain, love everlasting.
I never want to forget. Never want to let go.
The hurt reminds me that I love, and that makes
it worth all the pain.

Waiting on My Tiger

You reach a point where you
just can't.
Immobile, sitting in a bubble, floating
through.
Watching madness surround, eyes
flooded in Dolby.
Making sense of nonsense.
Impossible.
Truths hidden, motives
malicious.
One can eat an elephant, a plane
even.
One bite to start the meal.
Planes and elephants
tangible.
The tiger refuses to lend his
tail.
On a throne sits a man, bearded and
judgmental.
Expects action opposite of how he
created.
Individuals, so individual, pretending
to be the same.
Knowing truth, living opposite to,
condemning others for how they

are.
Where do we start?
What defines greatness?
Is there not fault and error in every great
mind?
So I sit, waiting on my tiger, some vision,
perhaps a guiding light.
One not so vague that I have to discern,
interpreting metaphors and
nonsense.
Perhaps this is the end, maybe the
beginning,
of something good or
terrible.

Stained

It hangs in his close,
not hers.
I use these pronouns not because of how we
think of
ourselves–
but because this is how we have been
identified.
That said, if I was offended, a small
courtesy, expected, demanded,
use ones that don't
offend.
Pronouns—used in absence of a proper noun,
my name, my identity, the way I know myself,
the way I am
known.
This is how a person can communicate,
with me,
with others.
Thoughts drift, avoiding the dress, the
wedding dress.
Once a powerful talisman, holding
great power,
beauty.
Mesmerizing the crowd,
as if something so

sacred
could be held together on nothing but silk and
thread.
Expensive, personal,
forgotten.
No longer pure, untouched like the
snow-covered hills outside
Anchorage.
Time and darkness pass, staining the
fabric.
Want, need, desperation, tell me to
wash.
As if soap and bleach can cleanse
feelings, actions, history.
I look, little peeks and glimpses, fabric
yellow and aged–
can actually feel the energy that once held joy,
tears,
dreams.
Not forgotten, so far removed, that reality no
longer
fits, exists.
Do we move on? Start over? Sit in
uncomfortable silence? Can we fix what
once was?
Life moves on, time passes, caring little
for the people that
experience it.

Entangled

Birds of a feather, red tail in the
wind.
They race in circles, dance with
love.
Consent in the air, notated in
posture.
Beams of Apollo applaud the
gesture.
Precision, grace, a touch of
insanity.
They unite, intertwining in a
free-fall.
Beautiful and dangerous,
unprotected.
Duality, unity, reckless, and
necessary.
Twigs crack, leaves fall, still
one being
Pain ignored, oblivion waits
patiently.
Climax achieved Father Time
smiles.
The grasslands wave in unison,
approve.
Success inches from a death's

embrace.
Separating to become dual, forever
united.
Eggs sit warmly, grass and branch
staged.
Guided by instinct, encoded in
DNA.
Life, love, reproduction,
the wait.
Life without risk, not worth
living.
Time without pain produces
nothing.

My Path to Destruction

The Bible says many profound statements.
Has many pages of words, metaphors, and
histories.
Ancient wisdom from the east that has been
transformed and organized in the west.
I've walked many roads, easy and hard.
Made as many mistakes as there are visible stars
in the sky.
One passage paraphrased from memory stands
out.
I think on it from time to time.
Can agree and disagree depending on the soil
my boots are currently traveling.
"Enter by the narrow gate; for wide is the gate
and broad is the way that leads to destruction,
and there are many who go in by it.
Narrow is the gate and difficult is the way which
leads to life, and there are few who find it."
I've walked so many roads, blazed trails into the
fires.
Know that these roads were not wide.
Never easy.
Always destructive.
There may be an easier way to destruction.
Faster paths to the inevitable.

I have yet to see them, know not of their
existence.
Perhaps the narrow and nonexistent roads I've
walked are wide in comparison.
And the truly narrow, so small that atoms barely
can pass through.
Perhaps the righteous must transfigure their
bodies into camels, then walk through the eye of
a needle.
Righteousness sounds like an absurd statement.
I have met no one that fits this description. Not
by definition.
Can't even imagine it as a destination.
Life, always volatile, a constant struggle.
There's a war going on. Outside, inside.
You see it in nature, in animals, insects,
biologically, atomically, from the depths of the
sea to the Stardust that stretches to infinity.
Creation always has destroyed to live. Death
creates life. The beauty is in the pain. The
struggle, the fight—that's the stuff that sustains
life.
There's truth in fiction, and a lot of fiction in
truth.
The ancients knew this, thought deeply, created
answers in mythology.
I know not where I'm going, but I will not stop
until I reach my destination.

A Moment in Divinity

There is much to have, little of
worth.
Expectations high, we measure,
judge, with a different tape.
We analyze results, actions,
failures.
Yet ourselves, wish to be seen through
a special set of eyes.
As if strangers see intent over the
obvious.
We love the earth. Wish to preserve it at
10 miles to the gallon.
Pack lunches in disposable plastic
bags.
Always chasing the next best
thing.
Measuring our worth in dollars
spent.
Selfish, narcissistic, the whole, the
group.
Yet see it only in others.
Unwilling to forgive, understand, extend
compassion.
Life is precious, a moment in divinity.
How dare we waste it!

Mephistopheles Takes the Throne

The light shines through a dark glass
Distorting droplets of an experiment
Skewing facts through propaganda
Fragmented truths in layered realities

Seeking shade from the whistleblower
Principalities sheltering agendas
Hysterical misrepresentation
Absurdities camouflaging missions

Little tin soldiers with backpacks
Tofu and cucumber sandwiches
Tucked away in anime lunchboxes
Marching off to public programming

The art of educational indoctrination
Breeding out the ability of free thought
Innovation rendered obsolete
Progress evolving to repression

Polarizing the infinite into binary
Woke enlightened and unaware
Black lives only mattered to people
Just another political charade

Desperate to keep your eye on the ball
Intricate deception with sleight-of-hand
While shoplifting our remaining liberties
A master web weavers dreamcatcher

I had a dream, but I can't remember
Intelligence becoming manufactured
The last men standing fade away
Mephistopheles claims the throne

The Duality of Man

The Duality of Man

The man within screams in silence
not in fear or anger but frustration and loneliness
always surrounded by people
drowning in the flood of the sea
a drop in the human bucket filled to the brink

The man shouts in a loud voice
consumed by intolerance
blind of his own clumsy footprints left behind
how could they be so stupid
the world just as blind and dumb and oblivious
as me

The man sees suffering in the world.
feels it in his heart as it shatters into billions of
pieces
the struggle ugly and desperate
the people deprived of dignity and grace
cruel intentions abound

The man greedy for another bite of the big apple
laces up and marches, oblivious to the little
people, trampled underfoot

they get what they deserve; they choose to be
that way
rape, pillage, take by force, because might is
always right

The man has forgotten we are mankind
where is the kind, tender touch
the fingertips of the gods that brush our cheeks
to wipe away a stray tear
how do we kill the devil and not damage the
divine
would we even know right if there was no wrong
pain and suffering, just a tool to help us
appreciate love and compassion
we are not gods; we are not devils
perhaps a touch of each lives in us all
to kill one would kill the other

The duality of man

Two Wings, One Bird

Left wing, right wing, matter not.
Separate appendages.
Same feathers, same bird.

Always at war.
Not the wings but the observers.
As if observation constitutes participation.

How can teamwork be seen as competition?
Can flight be sustained without cooperation?

If the viewer can't see the obvious. Wings are
not the birds. Will we ever identify the predator?

When day's end comes, does a hunter really cry
over the pains of the kill?
Does a lion feel empathy for a gazelle?

Living Infinite Realities

Living infinite realities
Many individual interpretations
A figment of someone else's
Imagined perceptions

Who am I to you
How do I portray myself
What do I reflect
What paradigm is received

Am I kind and affectionate
Shrewd and calculating
Blunt or a little rude
Perhaps obscene

Punctual dependable
Intellectual and wise
Unrealistic or detached
Perhaps criminally violent

Can I really be just a sum
Of thought and experience
Neatly folded and tucked
Filed away in a memory

Who gets to define
To decide, who's who
What's the criteria
The final word

Can I not be what I think
My feelings and imagination
Histories and futures
Do I not have a say in things

Fantasy

Sitting in a quiet little room
The perfect place for solitude
Comfort with the smell of loneliness
Sorrow and self-pity heavy in the air

Stale smoke staining the walls
A cigarette burning to the filter
Thoughts floating around
In a mind of senseless realities

An old clock ticking out the time
Hammering out the future
Beating each moment into submission
Forcing each second into being

And a man gasping each breath
Lungs starving for oxygen
Brain dying to be fed
Thoughts rolling around

Forever in the past
Reliving a made-up dialogue
Creating make-believe history's
Forever living in fantasy

One Breath

I wasn't, then I was

Nothing, empty, void

A thought, a smell, a breath

One breath

I am, I see

I feel, I crave

Hunger, thirst, greed

Experience, understanding

I share, I give, I love

I was, then I wasn't

One breath

Humanity

How beautiful we are
In our own disgusting way

Civilized, freethinking
Parasitic and destructive

We build, we paint, we war
Divine, yet beast-like

We destroy much
To create little

How beautiful we are
In our own disgusting way

A Place of Silence

Last night I woke up unaware
I just couldn't remember anymore
the smile that lifted my frown
that light bright enough to recharge my
brain with serotonin and oxytocin
like the moon, we traveled through many
changes
each phase left its special fingerprints
forever etched in history

how is this even possible
to become so comfortable in silence that you
forget to speak
time flying in fast forward as we sit in a quiet
room
then waking up one day to realize that you don't
even know me
can't stand me even
but somehow are madly in love
with an idea
some imagined creation
that was born in the silence

I knew for a long time
heartbreaking more and more each day

until finally I picked up a broom and swept
up the remaining pieces in an attempt to
share them with someone else
desperate to recreate a feeling
anything
to remind me of youthful lust, love, and
adventures
perhaps turn the shards and dust back to
clay
something moldable and soft as a newborn's
tender heart

I should have done many things
many things I shouldn't have done at all
but how could I sever the bond between
two living strangers
I wanted my cake eaten and whole
deceptive only for your protection
crushing when discovered

and now we stand
divided in a kingdom left in rubble
we walk alone in a desolate future
the past sparkles and tempts
but walking in history's footprints
will only return us to a place of silence

I Never Wanted to be a Poet

45

I never wanted to be a poet.
Poetry sucks.
I mean, who thinks they can get rich writing
poetry.
No one.
The only people that read poetry are poets.
Well, perhaps a few others, people that feel.
People that see the world differently.
Think differently.
And then.
Life.
I've lived many lives.
Died and been reborn too many times.
Trauma and pain etched into my heart and soul.
Scar tissue built out of self-preservation.
The great wall that every survivor builds around
their heart,
their mind.
Sometimes to keep things out.
People, memories, pain.
Other times to keep things in.
People, memories, feelings.
Maybe just to hold on.
Fingers forever gripping the tiniest thread.

Hope, sanity, the last marble before it rolls onto
the floor.
Each life brings a new perspective.
I begin to see with new eyes.
Find pleasure in the pain.
Potential in the chaos.
Beauty in simplicity.
Therapy.
Sure, I've had a few pharmaceutical cocktails.
Been practiced on by doctors.
Nothing worked.
So I write.
Always wanted to write.
Books and songs, not poetry.
I've done both, neither one as therapy.
The pen drags across the paper.
Drips the pain and beauty and feeling I can't
express verbally.
Thoughts that are non-linear, emotions and
pictograms.
I release them there, filed away, notepads in a
cardboard box.
Rubbish mostly, not meant to read.
Not by me, and certainly not you.
Nothing lyrical, no meter, no verse.
That's what poetry was to me.
Dr Seuss.
A sing-song of rhyme committed to memory.
A talent.

And then I discovered poetry.
Free verse.
Just people expressing.
Anything.
Whatever they feel.
Dripped out however they shape it.
Prose no longer necessary.
Just beauty, tragedy, protests of the heart,
injustice.
I read and read.
Understood, felt, cried, laughed.
No wonder poets read poetry.
Who else could relate and understand.